MYOB

mind your own brand

A collection of articles by Dave Lubelczyk

Presented by **IMAGE**identity, LTD

This book is dedicated to my wife, my kids and my entire family. Without their love, support and inspiration, I would not be able to follow my dreams each and every day.

MYOB

Contents

Afterword

Introduction:
Ready for your adventure?

This book is a collection of articles I published on
mindingyourownbrand.com. Each one is a separate piece
designed to make you think differently about how
you manage your brand. For this book to be effective, you do not have to read it page-by-page from
cover-to-cover. Think of it more like the 80's children's
books which allowed you to "choose your own adventure" and determine your own fate.

Begin by choosing a random article that piques your
interest and read it. At the end of each article, spend
some time thinking about how this could help your
business. Ask yourself "What I am doing (or not doing)
in my organization and how can this concept help me
strengthen my company's brand?"

After that, choose your adventure by asking yourself
"Is there something I can do to deepen my company's
relationship with those who come in contact with my
business?" Finally, develop and write down a plan
to implement this organizational improvement and
strengthen your brand. Set a timetable in which to
execute the plan and live by it.

Repeat this process often. If you do, you will develop a
habit of constant organizational improvement which is
essential to building and maintaining the extraordinary
brand culture necessary for long-term success.

Daddy, what do you do at work?

One morning at breakfast, my four-year-old asked me what I do all day at work. As I started to give my thirty-second elevator pitch that I use at networking events, I soon realized he didn't care how "I build stronger brands and improve organizational dynamics" nor did he seem interested in how "I help companies succeed."

So I told him that "I make companies better." And he asked, "Are they sick?"

"Well kind of," I answered, struggling to bring my complex methodology of creating extraordinary experiences and advocacy building down to a single phrase that would satisfy my son. Finally I said, "I make stores, restaurants and banks into fun places to shop and work." Satisfied with the answer, he shifted the discussion to something more important; what we were going to do together that day.

As I later pondered this discussion, I realized that we often describe our businesses in terms of how we understand them, not in terms our audiences will relate to. My son understood 'fun' was better than 'not fun' and he has often been bored in stores, restaurants and banks. By putting things in his terms, he was able to personally relate to that description and see why making them fun would be a good thing.

I have since changed how I describe my business and so should you. When you discuss your business, do not use industry jargon, fancy marketing phrases or well-crafted elevator pitches. Talk to the prospect in terms of their business and their issues. Which means you must ask them about their business and listen to their issues *before* you ramble on about your business.

If you are able to talk in terms of their perspective and are able to make a real connection between their business and your product, soon you will be spending some quality time together building a solid relationship.

Do you come here often?

Developing a long-term customer relationship is very similar to dating. How you grab a prospect's attention is critical. Advertising, direct mail, public relations, or a website may be the first step towards starting the relationship, but don't let your marketing effort be another tacky pick-up line. What you say and how you say it will determine whether the prospect will be interested in starting a relationship or respectfully decline your offer to have a drink.

Getting the prospect to meet with you is only the first step in the relationship building process. Taking the relationship to the next level requires your marketing effort to make an impression that will create interest and have them call you the next day. However, it is not about tricking the prospect into being interested. Don't make them think your first date will be a magical evening of dining aboard your private jet and dancing in Paris when you know you are only able to take them out for fast food. Make sure you are able to provide one hundred percent of what you claim and that they are expecting an experience you can provide. Otherwise, there will be no hope for a second date.

You may spend significant resources developing marketing materials to spark interest and get you that first date, but don't forget that your prospects are also judging your company by everything you say and do. Once the prospect walks through your door, you must take

5

great care to create an experience that resonates with the prospect and meets their expectations.

Instead of focusing on just marketing to develop the relationship, you must continually devote the resources necessary to examine all aspects of your business in order to determine what is adding to or subtracting from the experience needed to build a lasting relationship with a prospect. If you want this potential loyal patron to become more than a prospect, you need to do everything you can to ensure that they have an extraordinary experience each and every time they are with you.

If you develop a meaningful relationship based on trust while providing consistent experiences beyond expectations, your cash register will be ringing — just like church bells — to celebrate the relationship's success.

What are you going to name it?

My wife and I had our second baby, and like all expect-
ant parents we had to go through the often difficult
process of picking a name. Choosing a name is one of
the first big decisions you make for your child and it
can have a large impact on their future. Anyone familiar
with the 1980s movie *The Sure Thing* remembers the
diatribe of John Cusack's character in which he express-
es his disgust for the name "Elliot" who will grow up to
be "a fat kid with glasses who eats paste." He then goes
on to explain that "You gotta give him a real name. Give
him a name! Like Nick….Nick's a real name! Nick's
your buddy. Nick's the kinda guy you can trust."

Choosing a name for your company or product is as
important as naming your child, so don't take it lightly.
First and foremost the name has to be unique. Growing
up in classrooms filled with Davids, Johns and Jenni-
fers, the one thing that set me apart was my last name.
Speaking of my last name, that brings me to the next
point. You have to be able to say it and spell it. I know
first hand how having a name like Lubelczyk, which is
both difficult to say and spell, can be a real pain. In this
world of URLs, search engines, and online directories,
being able to spell your company's name is crucial unless
you want to spend a lot of money registering all the
misspellings of the name. Before you pick a name, make
sure you can get the .COM because chances are if you
can only register the .NET, the .BIZ or you have to put
in a lot of dashes or an "e" in front of it, no one will ever
find you...but they will find your competitor.

MYOB

A name also has to fit the personality of the company now and the personality you want it to grow up to be. Unlike Little Rickey who can become Richard the CEO or Rick the Fireman, you are stuck with that name for a long time. So choose wisely. If you have to change it later, the costs both financially and in lost recognition will be massive. The longer you have a name, the harder it will be to change. Just ask KFC who has recently gone back to Kentucky Fried Chicken because despite massive amounts of advertising telling us that KFC was their name and it stood for "Kitchen Fresh Chicken", no one really forgot that this company southern-fried their chicken.

Another thing to remember when picking a name is to avoid trendy names, names based on a fad, names that include current technology, or names that expire. Let's face it, does anyone get the latest electronic equipment at the Hi-Fi Shack or Computers 2000? I don't know many people who still want to go to the Cineplex, the Roller Disco, or the Bowladrome. These all may have been great names "in the day", but now they seem dated and irrelevant. So unless your company offers a retro theme or wants to forever stay in a time warp, avoid these names at all cost.

A popular naming trend is the use of only initials. This comes from the success of companies like GE, IBM and AT&T. But unless you're a "Blue Chip" company, this is probably not a good idea. Not many people want to buy from EDP NOW nor do they see ABC Office

Supplies as unique. I can't even guess what ADSP Inc. sells. Finally, AAA Computer Repair may get you the first listing in the phone book but does it really differentiate your service?

My entire family had very strong feelings about what the baby should be called and your company's stakeholders do too, therefore you must choose wisely. Always remember to consider if the name is appropriate, will people be excited about it, does it sound good, will people relate the name with the products or services you offer, and is it the type of company name people want to associate with. If all else fails, ask for help. There many good companies who specialize in developing the perfect name for your business.

For anyone who is interested, the baby's name is Nickolas and even though John Cusack had very little to do with the name, I hope my son grows up to be a buddy, the kind of guy you can trust, not someone who eats paste.

MYOB

After all, isn't it just a piece of toast?

If you have been on eBay lately you may have discovered the large number of pieces of toast for sale that "miraculously" bear the image of everyone from Jesus to Michael Jackson. This phenomenon is not new. Over the years, late night comedians have had guests with presidential potato chip portraits and vegetables shaped like Buddha. If you think about it, haven't we all seen a little bit more than the obvious in our food or in the clouds? I grew up with wood paneling in my bedroom and I had a number of faces and animals that hid within the wood grain. But when all is said and done, should we really get that excited when Mother Teresa appears in a cinnamon bun? After all, aren't people reading a little too much into things by declaring this a miracle and encouraging people to make a pilgrimage to see it?

Much like these over exaggerated interpretations, corporate logos are often designed to represent much more than their surface appearance. Throughout my career, I have been involved in a number of logo design projects. During the process, the company's leaders give a list of attributes they wish the logo to convey. The design team then spends long hours trying to find the right iconic imagery, type treatment, and colors which send the proper message. Every detail is scrutinized and in the end the perfect logo is unveiled to the public with much fanfare.

Recently the "New" AT&T unveiled its logo and the press release described the re-branding like this:

> *"The revitalized mark symbolizes these attributes — innovation, integrity, quality, reliability and unsurpassed customer care."*

> *"The new logo reinvigorates the AT&T globe — one of the most recognized corporate symbols in the world. The new globe is three-dimensional, representing the expanding breadth and depth of services that the new AT&T family of companies provides to customers, as well as its global presence."*

> *"Transparency was added to the globe to represent clarity and vision. Lowercase type is now used for the "AT&T" characters because it projects a more welcoming and accessible image."*

It is all well and good to want to develop a logo which represents the attributes of a company, but the real question is will the employees, stake holders, and customers really see it. More importantly, if they do see the logo as representing those things, will the company live up to the logo's promise or will it be just another marketing message which is undermined when some-one interacts with the company and discovers a less than extraordinary experience.

While the proper logo is important, companies must remember a strong brand is more than just a good logo. The companies brand is a reflection of everything they say and do, both inside and outside the organiza-tion. Therefore proper brand development must go beyond the creation of visual identities and market-ing materials. The entire organization must work to develop extraordinary experiences which create loyal internal and external advocates who are passionate about the organization.

Finally, we must remember that sometimes a logo is just a logo and a piece of toast is just a piece of toast. But for those of you who disagree, there is a french-fry shaped like the NIKE logo on sale right now on eBay.

Does your baloney have a first name?

Most of you probably answered O-S-C-A-R, but your baloney is most likely named O-N-S-A-L-E. The reality is that even though we all know the jingle, very few of us actually buy the product.

Every day companies spend millions of dollars on clever ads, catchy jingles and other ways to capture our attention all in the name of building brand awareness. Most companies feel that brand awareness equals brand strength. The theory is that if the company has someone's top of the mind awareness (the first name to pop into someone's mind when they think about a product category), then the person will faithfully buy the company's products.

We know the tag lines, we laugh at the ads, we all sing along with the jingles, but are we loyal to these companies? Probably not, and in most cases we do not even buy these products. A few years back, millions loved to say WASS-UP? but few ever bought the beer.

Recently, I spoke with one local business owner who spends a quarter of a million dollars each year on radio advertisements which he can not directly link to a single sale. When I asked him why, he replied "I am building brand awareness. I am making sure they know who I am, so when they need me they will call." The real question is ...will they?

MYOB

I grew up on Cape Cod and each year I knew summer had arrived when I heard the Thompson's Clam Bar song. As I write this article the tune is playing in my head, but in the 25 years I lived on Cape Cod I never once took route 28 to the clam bar sign for the tastiest eating from noon to nine.

The notion that brand awareness guarantees brand loyalty is flawed logic. Companies often point to the popularity of these "brand building" ads and call them a success saying "everyone knows who we are and they love our ads." But awareness doesn't mean guaranteed sales let alone brand loyalty. Just because we know all the lyrics to a local glass company's ad doesn't mean we will call them when our windshield is broken.

Even though awareness is important at the early stages of brand development, it is a very small part of building a successful brand. In order to create true brand loyalty you must develop a meaningful relationship with your potential customers. If this relationship is based on trust and you provide your customers with consistent experiences beyond their expectations, you will be able to recruit loyal advocates. These loyal brand advocates will share the company's vision, care about its success, see the company's products as the only logical choice and spread the word to others.

Therefore, building a lasting relationship with people who become your advocates is the only way to long term brand success. If you think that awareness alone will get you there then you are full of B-O-L-O-G-N-A!

Do you have a spine?

During the "60-second commercial" portion of a networking event, a chiropractor gave his laundry list of chiropractic services. Then he ended his commercial with the phrase, "Do you know someone with a spine? I can help them." Everyone laughed and said it should be easy for him to find business "except maybe in Washington."

Even though the population of people with spines is very large, the ability for him to acquire business may be harder than one might think. While everyone in the room knew people who "qualified" to be his patient, including themselves, the question that still lingered in their minds was who is an ideal patient to refer to the chiropractor? Because of that question, he will receive few referrals.

The chiropractor's lack of a specific target customer made his message too generic. He did little to connect his services to a particular audience's needs. He therefore left people wondering what area does he specialize in, why is he different, why should someone go to this chiropractor instead of someone else, and most importantly why are his services important to me or someone I know?

Many companies, like this chiropractor, are trying to be too many things to too many people. They assume the wider the audience the more likely their brand will succeed. These companies consider everyone a possible customer. When it comes to reasons to buy, they are often relying on the potential customer to fill in the dots. Even though these companies spend a considerable amount of time telling us what they can do and how they do it, the customer never sees specific reasons to consider the company's product nor why they should buy from that particular company.

Companies need to focus on matching up with a narrow group of "the right people" and to stop watering down the organization's offerings and messages to appeal to the masses. By understanding who the organization best matches up with, companies can better identify potential advocates who fit the ideal target profile.

Once a company has established a list of ideal target customers, it can begin to examine the specific products and messages those customers are looking for. The company then can construct offerings, create extraordinary experiences, develop true relationships and build passion amongst those customers. This will make it easier to recruit and retain loyal brand advocates.

So instead of marketing to everyone with a spine, spend some time profiling the right people to do business with and develop products and messages which exceed expectations and turn these people into fans of your organization who will do everything in their power to see that your organization succeeds.

MYOB

Do you love me?

As The Contours' song says, "Do you love me, now that I can dance?"

Why wouldn't you love them? They can Mash Potato...they can do the Twist.

Companies both big and small sing their version of this song everyday. We have the best quality...We offer the finest service... We will give you the lowest prices...Do you like it like that?

The answer is yes, we all like it like that. However, when the company asks if we love them and want make a long-term commitment to being a loyal customer; the answer is more like a line from a *Grease* song "Tell me more tell me more!"

Everyone is doing the Quality, Service, and Price dance. TV, radio and print ads are full of this message. So if you are focusing on these messages, you sound just like everyone else and therefore are invisible. The moral of the Quality, Service, and Price story is should you have it? Yes! These factors are a given and if you can't offer them you shouldn't even be on the dance floor. Should you use it to promote your company? NO!

But you say, "I do offer the best Quality, the best Service and I have the Lowest Prices. Why shouldn't I tell my potential customers?" Customers are looking for more. So what can you do?

Say something else!
Focus on an obscure aspect of your business and use that as a selling feature. Rhode Island's GEM Plumbing market themselves as "The Smell Good Plumbers!"

Do something no one else is doing!
Find innovative ways to use your product and market it to customers whom your competition hasn't even thought of tapping. A good example of this is The Mason Box Company, a jewelry packaging manufacturer who repositioned a portion of their product line for the funeral industry. They now market a line of custom bags and boxes for funeral parlors to return valuables and urns to loved ones.

Stand out on your dance floor!
Find ways to make buying from your company an extraordinary experience, like Jordan's Furniture who turned buying home décor into a family fun theme park adventure by adding motion rides, IMAX theaters, and restaurants to each of their stores.

Focusing on Quality, Service, and Price to market your company is as irrelevant as doing the Mash Potato and the Twist in a techno dance club. Instead, find a unique way to stand out from the crowd if you hope to build a lasting relationship with a prospect. If you do it right, they will love you even if you can't dance.

How low can you go?

While judging a freshman business plan competition at a local university, I noticed a pattern. Each of the student groups said they were developing a premium brand, but they would use a low-cost penetration pricing strategy. Even though they were often selling at a loss, they explained that by entering the market as the low price leader they would gain market share, people would fall in love with their product and they could raise their prices once they had built customer loyalty.

I could not think of any company that after entering the market with low-cost pricing, went on to be a dominate premium brand and could command an above market price. So, as a judge, I reminded them that "using this logic, they will develop a commodity level brand with very little loyalty and being a commodity is a hole few companies could ever hope to dig themselves out from."

I know what you're saying, "they are freshman and have a lot to learn about business." Hopefully these students have learned from this and will think differently when it really counts. However, this flawed thinking is not reserved for the business school novice because most companies can't get it through their thick skulls that a low-cost pricing strategy doesn't work and does not build customer loyalty.

Big box store "low-price guarantees" are creating a marketplace full of people who are fixated on price. Customers are no longer loyal to most brands and will switch from their "favorite" brand for a few pennies. These customers are loyal to low-price, not a particular brand. Because loyalty cannot be based on price, I would much rather see a company say that they were 10% higher than their most expensive competitor and then prove that they are well worth the price. This is a better positioning strategy than to bow to the unprofitable pricing practices that the current marketplace demands.

The only companies who have escaped this madness are the ones that realized a low-cost pricing strategy will never lead to long-term brand success. Once they stopped worrying about how competitive their price is and started focusing on their brand experience, they have now avoided being a low-cost provider and have a better chance at gaining customer loyalty. By doing this, they are seen as a premium brand which attracts true passionate advocates and builds a lasting relationship with their customers.

Customers will not become advocates if you have lured them in with a low-cost pricing strategy. The only true way to build advocacy is to find a unique way to stand out from the crowd by providing extraordinary brand experiences. Unless you provide an extraordinary brand experience, customers will see you as a commodity and will lack brand passion. Advocacy only comes from people who create a true relationship with the brand and that loyalty is priceless.

Have you perfected your Slinky technique?

By Guest Columnist Kristen Collins

Editors Note:
This article was written by an IMAGEidentity intern as her final project. I decided to share it with my readers.

Rummaging through an old toy chest, I stumbled across a neon pink Slinky with some of its rings stretched out from overuse. I reminisced on my child-hood years, remembering the frustrations I felt as I poked and prodded the slinky to glide down my 14 steps, only to watch it tumble down and land in a heap at the bottom landing. With each attempt, I grew more and more irritated by the imperfect efforts at using my slinky. My push was too soft, landing the slinky two steps below its starting point. My push was too hard, forcing my slinky to lurch off path into a rolling ball of chaos. Despite my exhausting efforts, my envy grew as I witnessed my younger brother gracefully slink the plastic toy down 14 stairs, landing in a pose that would surely score a ten amongst judges.

As these thoughts wandered through my mind, I began to link my previous frustrations as a child to those felt by small businesses and large corporations today. As a company seeks to develop its brand, executives may wonder "are we trying too hard?" "Will our custom-ers recognize our brand?" Yes, there does exist such a thing as trying too hard. As seen by the 50's toy slinky, a push too forceful could land a company in a jumbled heap of trouble. It is essential for a company to recognize its niche and develop its path to excellence. Specialization enables a company to focus their branding efforts and effectively target an appropriate market. By over-extending their brands and trying to make them stand for too much, a company may lose its sense of purpose.

Too many product lines which try to be everything to everybody very rarely produce effective results for companies. Rather, they find themselves questioning their missions, goals and company intents. Customers look at the company and see a mere chaotic and undefined purpose. Do you want your company to be the slinky laying in a tangled pile on the lowest level? Or do you prefer to be the slinky on which every company, employee, and customer focuses as you stylishly and consistently display your perfection.

As I glanced down into the stretched plastic, I could only envision my endless attempts at perfecting the art of slinky. While it did take quite some time, my efforts proved to be a success. Once I positioned my toy in the correct pose, angled at the perfect degree, the slinky managed to slide down the stairs as if it were a gold medal gymnast. My feelings of accomplishment mirror the feelings of achievement felt by companies as goals are completed and higher platforms of success are reached. Through specialty and pinpointed niches of the market, a company may find its very own path to slinky-stardom. After identifying the true purpose and mission of the company, customers will identify and emotionally connect with the company offerings.

How will you know when you have perfected the Slinky technique? You'll witness your slinky effortlessly float to the final platform, echoing its melodious rhythm on each step of the way.

Can they squeeze your toilet paper?

Mr. Whipple taught us that not all toilet paper is the same. Because of him, we all demand fluffy soft tissue instead of thirty-grit janitorial supply sandpaper for our bathrooms at home. However, when we enter a public toilet, things are not as predictable and we have come to expect very different bathroom experiences when we enter a restroom stall. From gas station restrooms to lavatories in five star restaurants, we have certain toilet tissue expectations when nature calls. Whether they know it or not, how a company lives up to those expectations is shaping our brand loyalty.

Companies spend significant resources developing logos, corporate identity standards, marketing materials, and loyalty programs but often forget that something as small as a three by three square of bathroom tissue is shaping their brand. A brand is more than just a logo; it is reflected in everything a company says and does. Consequently, something as "insignificant" as toilet paper can convey a great deal of information about an organization.

When developing a long-term brand strategy, it is necessary for organizations to examine all aspects of their business. Instead of just focusing on the marketing and corporate identity programs, they must consider that every point of contact between their company and potential audiences is affecting the status of the organization's brand. Companies must understand their audience's expectations and use that information to build brand experiences which strengthen a customer's relationship with the brand.

Building a successful brand means building a lasting relationship with people who become your advocates. If you provide your customers with consistent experiences beyond their expectations, you will be able to recruit loyal advocates. These loyal brand advocates will share the company's vision, care about its success, see the company's products as the only logical choice and spread the word to others. So with that in mind I ask you, can they squeeze your toilet paper and more importantly, will it exceed their expectations?

What did you expect?

A long time ago, back before I met my wife, I went on
a very interesting blind date. Well, it wasn't technically
a blind date. It was more of a set-up. I knew what Sara
looked like but that was all. She worked in another
department and a co-worker of ours decided to play
cupid because they knew we would "be perfect for each
other." Sara and I had a very brief hallway conversation
about when we should go out and what we should do.
I was excited to hear she liked my idea of trying a new
restaurant that had just opened up and we made plans
to meet there for dinner.

I had a lovely evening planned: dinner, drinks, a club,
and maybe if I was lucky, a romantic walk on the beach.
Instead, the night was a disaster from the minute we
opened the menu. You see, Sara was a vegetarian and
we were eating at Cape Cod's newest steak house.
There was literally nothing she could eat on the menu.
I offered to leave but she was a good sport. Sara picked
at her "side" salad while we discussed our lives and discovered how truly incompatible we were. In my mind
I had planned a truly extraordinary evening that in the
end was utterly dreadful for my date. After dinner she
thanked me for my well meaning effort. We said our
goodbyes knowing we both wanted different things out
of life; we definitely were not "perfect for each other"
and that was ok. I learned a valuable lesson about
expectations and the importance of asking questions.
en examining expectations, don't rely on assumptions
… ASK!

MYOB

Like the promise of new love, most companies are so smitten with the potential for new business that they fail to ask "does this prospect's expectations match up with the company's expectations." Because of this, they often build interactions that satisfy the company's needs and what they assume will impress the customer. However, in order to achieve brand success companies must understand expectations of all parties and if the alignment is not there, they must walk away.

By asking questions of both the prospect and themselves, companies can understand the expectations on both sides. They can then determine if there is a true fit and weed out the people who are misaligned before either party walks away with a bitter taste from the inevitable bad breakup. More importantly, when this alignment does exist it is easier to build an interaction that is truly extraordinary for both parties.

If your company wants to build brand advocacy, don't try to be everything to everyone. Instead, match up your company's expectations with each potential advocate's expectations, otherwise your customer may wake up one day and say "I think we should see other people because this is just not working."

If they come, have you built it?

Every time I watch television I see ads which depict the most wonderful places to shop. One particular ad depicts a home improvement superstore full of friendly, helpful, knowledgeable staff in every department. The ad goes on to explain how this staff is there to assist you in every facet of home improvement and repair. One day I needed a part for my kitchen faucet and a new cordless drill, so I set out for that store.

Upon arrival the only person who acknowledged my presence during my first ten minutes in the store was the "greeter" who was trying to get me to fill out a credit card application. The staff who were standing in the plumbing aisle shuffled me to the next person who "knows more about this department." After talking to three associates and spending fifteen more minutes searching, I finally bumped into the fabled "plumb-ing expert' who would know just what part I needed. Unfortunately he was new and the "other guy" who "knows all this stuff" was not here today. He pointed me to where I could look for the part on my own and "maybe be able to figure out what is needed."

After wandering around the store for thirty minutes, I left empty handed and frustrated. I ended up buying my part and the drill at the small local hardware store.

Why is it that companies paint such a wonderful pic-ture in their ads only to disappoint the customer when they come to shop? It is not only the big box stores who do this. I recently read an ad for a local home heating company claiming that they "provide superior

29

personalized service." This was the same company who gave me the runaround when I first tried to set up my fuel contract. They told me "the person who handles that is too busy" to take my call and to "call back tomorrow morning when they might have more time." In that case, I went with one of the "big boys" and I have been very pleased with the service.

Either big or small, my point is that if you say it in your ad make sure you can and are delivering it 100% of the time or else you are setting your current and potential customers up for a big disappointment. A disappointed customer may or may not come back, but either way they will talk and tell everyone about their negative experience.

Wouldn't it be better to exceed the expectations you set out in your advertising and have the resulting word of mouth advertising be positive? As the line in the movie *Field of Dreams* goes, "if you build it, they will come" — if it is extraordinary, they will tell their friends. After all, word of mouth advertising is the most effective form of promotion, especially if it expands the reach of your paid advertising.

Companies must remember that the first rule of setting expectations in your advertising is

— If they come, have you built it?

Why can't they see it?

While browsing at my library's used book sale I came across a book of Magic Eye images. As I flipped through it I remembered this early 90's fad when these images dominated shopping mall kiosks, poster shops, Sunday comics and coffee table books. I also remembered the first time I tried to see the hidden image amidst the swirls of colors. Everyone who could see the magic 3-D object couldn't understand why I was having so much trouble. It was obvious to them and they would shout out hints on how to see it like, "Let your eyes cross, blur your vision, then refocus". For the longest time, nothing seemed to work. After staring at the image for a short eternity, I finally saw it. Then, because I was used to seeing the 3-D object, I couldn't see anything but the hidden image. Most people were eventually able to crack the code but there were a few people, like my grandfather, who either gave up trying or said they saw it just to shut everyone up. After re-living this perception-based fad, I began to reflect upon the concept of perception and the role it plays in building brand advocacy.

Our expectations plus our past experiences effect how we see a situation and because of that we often do not perceive things the same way others do. Like the people who cracked the Magic Eye code, companies and their employees are often so close to their products, service, and culture that they often perceive interactions very different than their customers. Because of this, companies and their employees may feel they offer the best products and services in the world, but if customers don't perceive it as the best and it doesn't meet their expectations, then it is a crummy offering.

To an employee who is close to the company's everyday inner workings, a customer problem may seem routine, no big deal, and something that just happens. The employee may see the issue as something that "just slipped through the cracks" or had been the result of a process "the company fixed or can easily fix now." Employees often perceive a customer issue as the result of "one bad apple", and they often say "we have a procedure for that, but one person just didn't follow it."

Because of their familiarity with the company, an employee's perception of a customer's issues may be that the customer is harping on the negative and needs to move on. But for a customer, THEIR ISSUE is not routine and they don't know the company fixed the process, protocol, etc. Until proven different, that one bad experience five years ago is reality for the customer, even though many of the things the customer recalls as being negative may have been fixed or no longer happens now. Even if their current issue is unrelated, they think "here we go again." The customer's perception is based on THEIR past experience which is all that they have to go on. Therefore THEIR experience is REALITY: one bad employee is ALL of the company's employees and it is not just limited to employees; this goes for product quality, pricing, customer service, support hold times and so on.

So how does perception play into building brand advocacy?

Every time a customer interacts with your company, if you don't provide and experience which they "perceive" as extraordinary, they will remain passive if you're lucky. They will stay that way until some other interaction changes their status either up or down.

However, if the interaction doesn't work for the customer and they expect something you can't deliver, they will be a detractor. This means they will tell the whole world how bad they perceive you to be.

On the other hand, if your company cultivates a culture which understands customer expectations and perceptions, you can ensure that every customer has an extraordinary experience each and every time they interact with you. Because of this, your company will build passion in your customers and recruit advocates who will tell the world just how extraordinary they perceive you to be.

So if you find yourself saying, "We are such a great company, why can't our customers see it?" Then ask yourself, "Are we giving customers an experience that they perceive is extraordinary?" If not, then ask "How can we build an organizational culture which understands expectations and provides brand experiences that people will perceive as extraordinary?"

Can I put you on hold?

I was put on hold the other day and as I waited for my customer service representative. I was treated to some lovely hold music as well as a message about the company which I had called. This message told me about their latest innovative products as well as how much they valued me as a customer. The message went on to describe how they were committed to customer service and encourage customer comments in order to improve their products and services.

I laughed as I listened because have been a customer of this company for a long time and I know that they provide some of the worst customer service, never want to make any changes to accommodate the customer, and their competition have been offering the same "innovative products" for a number of years. When the customer rep finally came on the line, I asked him about the disconnect between the message and reality. He said that he "didn't make the message; it was the owner's idea." I offered to talk to the owner about this dilemma, but the sales rep informed me it would do no good because "he'll do it his way no matter what." So much for valuing customer's opinions.

This small business is not the only company that fails to consider how their hold message will affect the customer on the end of the line. Everyday, companies are annoying and potentially losing customers due to the conflicting messages they are providing to the people on hold.

A great example of this is a company which was having a large number of reliability problems with one of their new products. This issue caused a high volume of calls to tech support. The company had recently added a promotional message to the hold system, talking about their new products and how reliable they were. Needless to say, this only enraged their already frustrated customers who were now reminded how "wonderful" their broken product was, two to three times during a hold session. By the time the tech support rep got on the phone, the customers were ten times more enraged then they were at the beginning of the call.

By now you may be saying, "My company is okay because we use a local radio station as hold music." Well, this can cause a loss in customers even faster. I was on hold one day with my car dealer waiting to schedule a brake job. As I waited on hold for what seem like an eternity, I heard a radio ad for another garage complete with a phone number. So I hung up, dialed the number and got an appointment right away. They are now my car mechanics.

When developing a long-term branding strategy, it is necessary for organizations to examine all aspects of their business. They must consider that everything they say and do is communicating a brand message and therefore must be taken into account. So when a company asks, "Can I put you on hold?" they should also ask themselves "Will the customer be there when we pick back up?"

MYOB

Why did the relationship end?

Recently a number of couples I know are getting a divorce. One relationship ended because one of them found someone who met their needs more than their spouse did and another marriage is ending due to lack of passion. A third couple is calling it quits not because of one particular issue, but instead because of a building up of many little things that went unresolved and turned into one big problem. In each case, one of the partners in the relationship didn't realize that things were that bad until it was too late and the relationship was beyond repair.

After thinking about these failed relationships, I realized that this is often the same situations that happen in business everyday. Customers sever ties with companies leaving owners scratching their heads wondering "what happened, I thought they liked us."

Each day, customers are leaving relationships with companies at rates that rival the national divorce rate. So what can companies learn form these divorcing couples that will help them retain customers?

Like the first couple, many companies feel they lose customers because someone better comes along. They think that with cheaper prices, more selection, or bigger advertising budgets, how can they compete? While on the surface this may be true, a customer's decision was probably not a snap one. Over time, the company failed to meet their needs one little thing at a time. Then "pool boy" came along and the customer fell deeply in love with this new company because it promised to fulfill every need and had cheaper prices, more selection, and better advertising.

The second couple's problems centered on passion. Passion is critical for customer retention, but that passion is not one-sided. Companies must also have a passion for their customers. They must appreciate them and strive to provide an extraordinary experience which fuels passion or else customers will leave for a younger, sexier company that ignites their passion.

Finally, the third couple offers a valuable lesson. Little issues that go unresolved can add up to big problems. Everything you say and do creates the customer experience, so be proactive and try to solve issues before they arise. Even proactive companies can't always be perfect, but they can offer extraordinary experiences when they aren't. If you mess-up, admit it and make the resolution of the issue an extraordinary experience. A problem moment can often be the best opportunity to "wow" a customer and gain them as a passionate advocate.

So work on your relationships each day and make every interaction extraordinary. If you don't, you may wake up one day to customers asking you for divorce.

MYOB

Does anyone know why Randy left this message?

"Who is Randy and why is he calling me?" was all I could think of as I retrieved my voicemail. He left no reason for calling, just "Hey Dave, it's Randy! Call me!" and his phone number. Despite the fact that I don't have any colleagues, clients, or friends named Randy, I still got the sense from the message that I should know him.

I felt there was a good chance he was someone whom I met through networking. So, I checked my database of contacts and my stack of recently acquired business cards with no luck. I Googled the number he left and the number that showed up on caller ID. I found out he called from the XYZ cleaning company. This tidbit of information confirmed that I did not know Randy, but still thinking someone referred him to me and intrigued by his cryptic message, I dialed the number.

After only 10 seconds on the phone, I realized that I definitely did not know Randy, he did not know me and I was just another name on his call list. As he immediately went into his canned sales pitch, I knew I would never be doing business with Randy or XYZ Cleaning Company. Like so many telemarketers, Randy had tricked me into talking to him and could care less if I truly needed his products or services. No matter how I objected to what he was saying, he countered with his scripted pitch and was insisting that I had to meet with his sales guy "who happened to be coming to my area."

Why do companies let this type of situation destroy their brand's image? In a matter of seconds, Randy had ruined the credibility of XYZ cleaning company and ensured that even if I needed a new corporate cleaning company, I would never use their services. The trick he was using got me to call him back and even got me to listen to his pitch, but his tactics, like so many other sales systems, ended up eroding the integrity of the company's brand.

A company's brand is shaped by everything that each employee in an organization says and does. Therefore, companies often try to preserve their brand by controlling all aspects of workers' action with systems and rigid scripts. But instead of having a positive effect, they are producing experiences that are less that extraordinary for the potential customer. Then corporate leadership can't understand why the company doesn't achieve the desired results and their brands are losing dominance in the marketplace.

So what should Randy have done differently? First, he should have never tricked me into calling him back. Second, once he got me on the phone, he should have asked me if this was a good time to talk. If the answer was "NO", he should have thanked me for my time and hung up with no further questions. This would have impressed me and added to the credibility of the brand.

If I did want to talk, he should have talked to me like a normal human being, not a robot programmed to counter my every objection and to make me agree to a meeting as early in the conversation as possible. This normal conversation would have allowed him to qualify me as a prospect and create a favorable experience for me.

Randy was the first person to begin my relationship with this company. If he had created an extraordinary initial experience, he could have moved me one step closer to being an advocate for this company's brand. Instead, he resorted to dishonest sales tricks to fill his calling quota and used a canned script which did little to peak my interest in XYZ's services. His overall tactics reflected poorly on the company's brand and should leave XYZ's leadership asking, "Does anyone know why Randy left this message?"

Do you have a big BUT?

My family and I went to a new restaurant for lunch. The food was great, the decor was very nice, the wait staff was friendly, BUT it took forever to get our order. They were extremely under staffed for the number of tables they were trying to serve. This simple problem made a potentially extraordinary experience less than ordinary. To make matters, worse the staff did nothing special to alleviate the pain of our unusually long wait and therefore they lost a possible opportunity to gain an advocate. Now if someone asks what I think of this restaurant, I will be hesitant to give a glowing review and if I do suggest this place, there will be a big BUT.

A person's perception of a company's brand is determined by everything that company says and does. Consequently even the most insignificant glitch can create a big BUT in a potential advocate's mind. Therefore, it is necessary for organizations to eliminate their BUT's by reviewing all areas of their business.

In doing this, you must remember that eliminating BUT's does not require perfection. No matter how hard you try, you won't always be perfect. Things don't always go as planned and people will make mistakes. Therefore, you must create an organizational culture which strives for extraordinary experiences not perfection. Within this culture your team will be able to handle any situation that arises in a way that is appropriate and extraordinary.

If an experience falls short of customer expectations, your team must be able to make up for it in an extraordinary way. If they only react in the expected way, customers will feel slighted and it will make a bad situation worse. Mistakes can be the best opportunity to create a memorable experience and missteps are often the best time to provide an experience which recruits an advocate.

Only if your team understands expectations, lives up to organizational standards, and eliminates the BUT's, will they provide customers with an experience that is consistent with the brand promise. By evaluating every point of contact between your company and potential advocates, you can then give your team the basic rules, expected outcomes, and the resources to get the job done. Armed with these tools, your team will be able to provide extraordinary experiences which eliminates the BUT's and therefore recruits loyal advocates.

Do you have a BUT? How big is it? What is it doing to the value of your brand? Is it keeping your company from recruiting advocates and being successful? If so, what are you doing about it?

So, what are you waiting for? Now is the time for you and your team to get off your butts and build a brand culture that eliminates your BUT's on a daily basis.

Why can't we be friends?

A graphic designer friend of mine sent me this email the other day with the header "Awesome Marketing Strategy":

When we got home there was a 9"x12"x4" box with the mail. The return address was a printer in Cranston, RI that I had heard about but never used. I opened the box and under a top layer of crinkled paper was a piece of their letterhead with this message:

> *"It's a safe bet that a passion for knitting may not be the only thing we have in common..."*

Attached to the note was a pair of 9", #10 bamboo knitting needles. A business card was tied to the needles. I teach knitting and have a couple of students with the same first name, but a quick visit to the printer's web site showed me an unfamiliar face. So I sent her an e-mail.

Long story short: this relatively new sales rep got my name, probably from their database, cruised my website and saw links to knitting websites.

I met her this past Wednesday and we had a wonderful conversation about knitting. She's really great and a go-getter. I think she will probably get my business when I have a printing job.

This was an "Awesome Marketing Strategy" for many reasons. First, the message delivery method was different which made her stand out in a pile of mail. Rather than send the typical envelope or a postcard, this sales rep sent a box, something that would stand out and would not be thrown away. This is a technique I have used myself and I often encouraged clients to "think inside the box" when it come to direct mail.

Why? Because a box guarantees your direct mail piece will be opened. Boxes, big or small, always end up on top of a stack of mail. Gatekeepers would never open a box addressed to someone else and the "little kid at Christmas" in all of us ensures that the intended recipient will be compelled to open a box to see what it is.

The second reason this was an "Awesome Marketing Strategy" was that her message was creative, compelling, and left the recipient wanting more. The rep wetted my friend's appetite and did not overwhelm her with capabilities brochures, samples or special offers. This marketing piece didn't try to do too much. It did what it was supposed to do; it introduced the company, the rep and extended an offer to begin a dialog. But more importantly, this piece made an offer to begin a relationship based on something other than doing business together.

This is great example of how to begin a *true* relationship with a prospect. Instead of just marketing *at* my friend, the rep marketed *to* her, while setting the stage for a potential friendship. By doing her homework, this rep found a basis for a friendship and who wouldn't want to do business with a friend? They now have something in common besides a potential order and when my friend needs a printer, she will call this rep.

So this rep has taught us how to stand out and catch a prospect's attention, but more importantly the lesson from this story is that instead of looking at a prospect in terms of just a sale, we should ask ourselves "Why can't we be friends?"

MYOB

Isn't it a small world?

Have you ever played the Kevin Bacon game? For those of you unfamiliar with the game, participants are asked to link actors back to Kevin Bacon with no more than six degrees of separation. Anyone who has played it quickly discovers how small Hollywood really is.

Like in the game, we often find ourselves asking isn't it a small world? Throughout our business and personal lives, we often say "I didn't know you went to high school with Bill" or "I just found out you are married to Sue." Few business people take advantage of how connected we really are and even fewer realize that if not managed correctly, this "connectedness" could hurt their brands.

A brand's strength can be measured by the number of passionate advocates a company have. These advocates believe in the brand and do everything in their power to see that the organization succeeds. The level of passion a person has is directly related to how extraordinary an experience they have had with the organization.

The main thing that most companies forget is that a person can be a passionate advocate or a bitter adversary even if they never use the company's products or services. This is why companies should provide extraordinary services to everyone who touches the organization, even if the interaction doesn't result in a sale.

A graphic design colleague of mine told me a story about how his neighbor's brother owned a very small property management company. The neighbor asked my design colleague to help his brother out. The brother had awful business cards and never could find a designer who produced the quality of my colleague's work. The designer was uninterested at first because it was a very small project and this client was definitely too small for his firm. But as a favor to his neighbor, he helped the brother out knowing full well he would never make any money on this project.

The designer resisted the temptation to "just bang this one out" and instead put considerable effort into the design. The resulting card was something the designer was very proud of and the brother was ecstatic. One day, the brother gave a card to a business associate. The person loved the card and asked who designed it. She was opening a chain of restaurants and needed a design firm. The brother passed on the design firm's name along with a glowing recommendation. Her restaurant is now one of this designer's largest clients.

Even though a person may not fit your business model or seems like a "small" customer, you never know who they may be connected to. Your willingness to help them find the answers to their problems, even if it isn't your product, will create a favorable impression in their mind. The experience you create will turn them into a fan of your organization and they will tell others about your company. Because you are never sure of how a person is connected, you should treat each and every person as if that experience could be the one interaction that makes or breaks your company.

In case you are wondering, I am only four degrees away from Kevin Bacon. I married Dr. Rebecca Ballard who, while working at Rhode Island Hospital, had an intern named Randy Fink. Before medical school, Randy was an actor who played the ER doctor in the movie *Philadelphia* starring Tom Hanks, and we all know Tom Hanks was in *Apollo 13* with... Kevin Bacon!

Why did they boo Damon and not Pedro?

Both left Boston on bad terms, both left for "better contracts", and both went to New York teams. So why upon their return, did Red Sox fans give Pedro Martinez a standing ovation and gave Johnny Damon a round of boos? I think Pedro summed it up best in his press conference, "Johnny put on the wrong uniform" and Red Sox Nation let him know it.

You will never find people more loyal, faithful, and passionate about a brand than Red Sox fans. Even though they were not winners for 86 years, fans stuck by this brand through all the high and the very low moments in this brand's history.

So why don't most brands induce this level of passion? Because most brands are not extraordinary. Unlike most brands, the Red Sox have always done things in an extraordinary way, whether it is a come from behind 2004 championship win or a heart wrenching 1986 World Series loss. Good or bad, this brand has always given fans something to be passionate about.

John Henry's group may own the team, but "Red Sox Nation" owns the brand. Red Sox Nation don't follow this team blindly; they have taken ownership of the brand and are committed to its success. Red Sox Nation are a group of brand advocates who cheer the victories, but also have no problem making it known when someone is not performing up to par. Based on fan reaction, Terry Francona said he thought his name was "You Suck" numerous times during his first season as manager.

A brand is more than just a logo or corporate identity. A brand is shaped by everything a company says and does, both inside and outside the organization. The strength of a brand is determined by the experiences surrounding the brand and how people feel when they interact with the organization. Therefore, companies must create extraordinary experiences and build brand cultures that inspire employees, customers and anyone who touches the company, to be passionate about the organization, take ownership of the brand and actively contribute to the brand's success.

Don't just settle for repeat customers, loyal patrons, or even plain old fans. Build extraordinary experiences and a brand culture surrounding your organization which inspires people to become advocates for your organization. Like the Red Sox, build

"{*Your Company*'s} Nation".

Have I resolved your problem?

I received an overdraft notice today. Not on my main account but on an account I haven't thought about in months.

This story began when some months ago I was convinced by a friend to open an account at his bank. You see, I haven't been happy with my "big bank" and I had been planning to move to a smaller, more customer-focused regional bank. The plan was to open the account with a minimal deposit and then transition my money over to the new account. But moving to a new bank account is a pain; you have to switch all the places that point to your account like bill pay, merchant account, and any automatic withdrawal like payroll. Needless to say, I was too busy and never got around to it. There was a "No Fee" period so I wasn't worried and I would get it moved eventually.

Time passed, I never used the account and I stopped opening the statements. That was until I received the overdraft notice. I guess the "No Fee" period had ended a few months ago and I had used up my balance with service charges. Now this account was costing me money and I had to do something about it. I called the customer service number and after the usual security questions, I told "Anna" my story. She looked up my record and confirmed my assumptions. Anna told me that if I went to a local branch and finally transferred my money, they could "probably" reverse the charges. I explained to her that my "local" branch wasn't so local (two towns away) which is part of the reason why

I never used the account. I had planned on banking mostly via the ATM, phone, internet or mail but I never found the time to set up remote banking or to move the money. Therefore, even though I still want to eventually switch to a new bank, maybe I should just close the account and set one up when I have the time to switch. Her reply was "Okay, please hold".

Upon her return, she informed me that she was able to "bring my account back to zero" and the account would be closed in three days. She then asked "if that is all" and in a scripted voice said, "Have I resolved your problem today?" I said "yes" but what I should have said was, "No, I still need a bank that cares about its customers and tries to build long-lasting relationships by providing products and services that solves their customers' actual problems."

This call illustrates a major missed opportunity that plays out everyday in most companies; customer service people who "solve" the problem at hand but fail to provide a larger solution that would deepen the relationship with the customer.

In this example, everyone and everything had done what they were supposed to do:

- the "No Fee" promo piqued my interest

- my friend convinced me to open the account

- the branch manager opened my account

- the system produced my monthly statement
- the system withdrew my monthly fee
- the system generated the overdraft notice
- Anna "resolved" my issue
- my account was closed

Did all the "transactions" happen correctly? .... Yes

Did each step go according to the script? .... Yes

Was the customer satisfied? .... I guess so

Did the experience make me an advocate? .... No

Even though I was "satisfied" with each step, not one person or system deepened my relationship with the bank and it definitely did not turn me into an advocate. Each step was a "success" but because they operated independently, the entire experience was a failure. I still wanted to leave my big bank but this small bank offered me no compelling reason to get off my butt, close the old account and set the new one up. Even when I called Anna and told her exactly why I was underutilizing my account, she followed her script and allowed me to slip away without even offering a way to make my transition to her bank easier. So much for the more customer-focused regional bank.

MYOB

In the beginning, this bank succeeded in making me a customer which is usually the hardest part. But instead of creating an extraordinary experience which would make me an advocate, they went through the motions and failed to keep me as a customer.

Do you really value my opinion?

As I mentioned in my previous article, I have been
unhappy with my "big bank". My main criticism of this
bank is that despite their advertising campaigns which
say that they are not your typical, big, uncaring bank,
over the past few years they have grown to a point
where they treat their customers more like a number
than a person. They no longer provide the personal
service they once did and now do not consistently live
up to their marketing promises. Therefore, when I
received an email with the subject line "We value your
opinion", I expected this to be a way for me to com-
municate my recent frustrations and provide them
with some constructive feedback. You can understand
my disappointment when I clicked the survey link
and a page came up which simply read "This survey is
closed." I felt as if the bank said "Well Dave, we value
some opinions but NOT YOURS."

I tracked down and called the person who had sent me
the email to give him my perceptions. He quickly dis-
missed me saying he had gotten the 200 responses he
needed. So I asked him why the email didn't say how
long the survey would be open, or why the link didn't
say something like "Thank you for your interest. Unfortunately the survey is now closed. If you would like
to contact us with any important comments, please call
or email us at..." I told him that his message really was
"We value the first 200 opinions, and then we don't
care." His response was that if I "really wanted to take
the survey" he could make that happen. He had missed
my point, and made me feel even less important.

MYOB

This is a perfect example of how companies can set up expectations which ultimately lead their customers to frustration. A brand is reflected in everything a company says and does. Consequently, something as "insignificant" as this survey page can send a strong message about how an organization values its customers. That coupled with unfulfilled advertising promises can quickly turn a potential loyal advocate into an annoyed adversary who will spread the story of their unfulfilled expectations to anyone and everyone who will listen.

When delivering a brand message, the important factor is not what you say but instead what matters is how they perceive it. Therefore, it is necessary for organizations to take a critical look at all aspects of their business and consider that every point of contact between their company and potential audiences is affecting the status of the organization's brand. Just by stating that you provide personal service and value your customer relationships is not enough. Companies must understand the expectations that these statements are creating and use that information to build an organization which provides experiences that strengthen a customer's relationship with the brand and not erode it.

If you provide your customers with consistent experiences which go beyond the expectations you create with your marketing promises, you will be able to recruit loyal advocates. However, this means that you must actually listen to what your customers have to say. Building a successful brand means building a lasting relationship with people who become your advocates. One way is to give them the proper tools to provide you with valuable feedback about your company. This will allow you to make changes in your organization and offer customer experiences which create a positive brand perception.

So with that in mind I ask you, do you really value your customer's opinion? Have you given them the proper tools to provide you with this valuable feedback? Are you actually listening to what they have to say?

MYOB

Why isn't every day
Customer Appreciation Day?

A few weeks ago, I went to a store and they were having Customer Appreciation Day. There were big posters in the window announcing the event and the store displays had signs announcing "special customer appreciation savings on select items." There was an unusual abundance of employees each dressed in a customer appreciation day tee-shirt and a "thank you" button. As I shopped, the staff were extra helpful with my questions and went out of their way to show me to the products that I was looking for. It was truly the best shopping experience I had ever had at this store.

However, as I began to check out, I listened to the interactions of the staff with other customers and the sentiment seemed forced. The sales associates were a little too eager to help, the manager opened a new register as soon as the line reached three people, and the cashier said "thank you" too many times for a normal checkout. It was as if they were competing with each other to see who could appreciate the customer more and in the end it all seemed extremely scripted. As I drove home, I began to feel that the day was less about appreciating the customer and more about getting people into the store to "take advantage of the customer appreciation savings on select items."

Even though most companies tout the incredible level of customer service they provide, in reality most of them offer a mediocre experience at best. Why is it that companies only appreciate the customers and provide extraordinary service when it involves adding to their bottom line?

Companies need to create a culture that truly values the customer and makes shopping an extraordinary experience every day instead of just on special sale days. I think back to the few situations where a sales associate went out of their way to truly help even though it may or may not end up in a sale. One that comes to mind was a story I heard the other day talking to a banker. He told me about a situation where he did not have a loan product to meet a small business owner's needs. But because he valued the relationship and truly wanted to help, he told the business owner that a bank across town had the perfect product for him. He even called ahead to explain the customer's needs and tell them he was coming.

Not only did this small but extraordinary gesture win over the small business owner who will likely come back to this banker for his other banking needs, but it also made the banker feel good about what he had done. This interaction gave both the banker and the small business owner a story they could tell others like myself in order to describe how his bank is different. They are now able illustrate how this bank is truly about providing service and how they value all business relationships even when the bank may not have the right products for you. This story shows that unlike the store, this banker truly appreciated the value of ALL customers, even those who don't result in a sale.

Companies need to cultivate a culture which develops true relationships, exceeds expectations and creates extraordinary experiences which build passion amongst both employees and customers. This passion will aid in the recruitment of advocates who will do everything in their power to see that the organization succeeds and because of this the company will ultimately achieve financial results. So, instead of only appreciating customers when there is a sale, why not make every day customer appreciation day?

Who is the MVP?

Baseball season has come to a close and the Boston Red Sox are the 2007 World Series Champions. Mike Lowell may have won the MVP, but he was definitely not the only candidate. David Ortiz put it best when during the celebration he exclaimed "I can't point to one guy that did this for all of us. It was everybody. That made it very special."

The team effort was also a highlight of Red Sox chairman Tom Werner's post-game comments. He talked about how he felt that it was a special win because every player was able to contribute in their own way. More importantly he talked about how the win wasn't just because of the team on the field. He felt it happened because of the efforts of the entire Red Sox organization. Werner went on to discuss how "it is a family which provides tremendous support to each other throughout the season." He added that "this family extends beyond the players and staff to the entire Red Sox community including the 6 million fans which make up Red Sox Nation." Later, team owner John Henry added his comments about how these fans were so important to the success of this team. He said "It is because of the fans we had the resources to hire top talent and put the best possible team on the field. That is why we are now World Series Champions."

Unlike the Red Sox who understand the important role the customer plays in their organization, many companies forget that the customer is the only reason the company exists. If the customer disappears, so does the resources to run the company. Everything we own is paid for by our customers and every member of an organization must remember that the customers not only pay the company's bills, they pay the employee's personal bills by way of a paycheck. Without them, we have no food, no shelter, no clothes, no car, and no vacations. Yet even though companies need customers, they often take them for granted and provide their customers with an experience that does little to build a connection to the organization and passion for the brand.

The Red Sox have built a brand culture that inspires customers to be passionate about the organization. Their fans take ownership of the brand and do their part to actively support the team. Because of this, the Red Sox are rewarded with extreme customer loyalty and the financial resources that go with it.

Your Most Valuable Player is your customer. So, like the Red Sox, don't just settle for repeat customers, loyal patrons, or even plain old fans. Build a brand culture surrounding your organization which recruits advocates and inspires people to actively contribute to your organization's success.

How can we thank you enough?

It's that time of year again. The holidays are upon us. The smell of turkey is in the air and Christmas carols have been echoing through the malls since the day after Halloween. It all adds up to one thing: holiday promotions.

With the economy as it is, businesses are trying harder than ever to move their bottom line away from Christmas RED and turn it into a profitable end of the year BLACK. This means that companies are doing everything they can to "give" unbelievable savings in order to "take" their customers' money.

But aren't the holidays supposed to be a time of pure giving; a time to say thank you to the ones who have helped us throughout the year; a time to appreciate what we have?

Not in the business world. The holidays fall during the fourth quarter which is when you need to make your bottom line as profitable as you can. With that in mind, most companies use the holidays as a way to drive up customer spending with promotions masked as holiday Thank You's. All too often, companies send holiday cards which are poorly disguised "Please Buy from Us" cards. Whether they are 10% off gift cards or offering a free gift when you bring the card into the store, these holiday greetings often say please more then thank you.

MYOB

We are taught from an early age that the "magic words" are "please" and "thank you". We quickly learn that as long as we are polite, we can use these phrases to manipulate others into giving us what we desire. Therefore most people miss the intended lesson and use please and thank you for selfish means rather than to be polite and appreciate the kindness of others. The words become less magical and we begin to only use them to get exactly what we want.

Ultimately, we have become jaded to the true meaning of please and thank you and what most never learn is that the true power of these words lies in the thank you not the please. If you give out genuine appreciation on a consistent basis people will feel a stronger bond to you and your relationship will truly deepen. Then when you do have to ask them please, they will gladly give you what you need.

So what can businesses do?

First, don't wait until the holidays to thank your customers, employees, vendors and anyone who helps your business succeed. Thank them throughout the year. Many small gestures of thanks go much farther than one at the end of the year.

Second, always try saying thank you many more times than you say please and remember to separate the thank you from your promotions.

Finally, give as much as you can before you ask for something in return. By giving without expectation you will truly reap greater rewards because you will build stronger relationships with people who will want to thank you for your kindness.

Happy Holidays and Thank You for being such devoted readers.

If the cake is bad, what good is the frosting?

At the end of a meal, I received a fortune cookie with a message that read "If the cake is bad, what good is the frosting?" After reading this fortune, I realized that I had discovered a phrase that summed up my entire brand development philosophy.

All too often, companies approach brand development by just worrying about the frosting. They spend all their efforts focused only on what people see on the outside (corporate identities, marketing messages, product and service positioning, etc.) Companies have trouble realizing that if they don't have the proper internal brand culture, customers may be wowed at first only to be disappointed by the bad taste that is left when employees deliver a less than promised brand experience.

In order to develop a strong external brand, companies must first develop a strong internal brand. By utilizing organizational development strategies along side brand development tactics, companies can create a brand culture which consistently delivers extraordinary brand experiences. The result is a brand which inspires passion and recruits both internal and external advocates.

Companies with strong internal brand cultures see increased revenue per employee and therefore greater profitability due to:

- Higher employee satisfaction

- Employee innovation

- Higher level of productivity

- Lower employee turnover

- Improved safety records

Because of the internal brand culture, each employee feels a connection to the organization. They become internal brand advocates who believe in the company and want to see it succeed. These advocates work to constantly improve and enrich the brand while they spread their passion to others both inside and outside the organization.

Strong internal brand cultures also lead to increased revenue per customer. This is due to the extraordinary external brand experiences that employees create which result in:

- Stronger customer relationships

- Higher customer satisfaction ratings

- Increased customer retention

- Larger number of customer referrals

- Better reputation in the marketplace

Companies who continually devote the necessary organizational development resources, consistently build and maintain strong brands. By focusing on the cake as well as the frosting, companies are able to ultimately achieve brand success by building internal advocacy.

MYOB

Instead of focusing on just external branding efforts, a combination of brand development plus organizational development is the proper recipe for creating an extraordinary brand.

Why can't I get that with whipped cream?

A few weeks ago, some friends and I were on our yearly trip to Nantucket. According to ritual we stopped by our favorite ice cream shop as soon as we got off the boat. My friend asked for whipped cream on his small cup of chocolate ice cream. The clerk proceeded to tell him that "whipped cream only comes with sundaes." Thinking it was a cost issue, he offered to pay the extra twenty-five cents that they charge to put candy on a cup of ice cream, which he felt would surely cover the cost of a squirt of whipped cream. The clerk refused the offer saying that was the "candy charge" and there is "no way" to charge him for just whipped cream. She went on to say that "the shop policy is that whipped cream can only be put on sundaes." So in order to get whipped cream. he would have to order a sundae with no hot fudge, no nuts and no cherry.

He settled for his chocolate ice cream without the added calories, but for the rest of the weekend we all had to listen as he told the entire island (or at least the half that would listen) how ridiculous this policy was. Needless to say, we did not pay a visit to that shop on our way back to the boat and it probably won't be our first stop on the island next year.

Small things can turn a basic interaction into an extraordinary customer experience or a massive disappointment. This story illustrates how a too restrictive policy hurt the clerk's chance to be extraordinary and ruined any chance of maintaining my friend as an advocate. All too often companies that claim to be creating better and more standardized customer experiences end up micromanaging their way out of customer loyalty by creating inflexible rules and policies.

Honestly, I don't know why the "no whipped cream" policy was in effect. Maybe it had something to do with inventory control, maybe the clerk didn't know how to ring it up because it was not a standard sale, or maybe the manager emphasized during training to only put whipped cream on sundaes. Whatever the reason, the clerk didn't feel empowered to solve the problem and create an extraordinary customer experience and therefore the policy hurt long-term customer loyalty.

Instead of trying to create specific rules which dictate how employees should act in all situations, companies must instead examine all aspects of their business and define broader goals and values which guide the organization. The company can then put employees in control of living up to these broader guidelines and encourage their staff to be responsible for determining what is adding to or subtracting from the customer experience and act accordingly.

The customer is NOT always right, but if you want to retain a loyal patron you need to do everything you can to ensure that they have an extraordinary experience each and every time they are with you. By outlining the broader goals and values for the organization to follow, the employees are able to interact with the customer in a way which seems right for the situation, instead of going through a predefined set of motions which does not fit the situation and will never result in a positive outcome.

MYOB

Would you dig through the trash for your customers?

Everyone is familiar with the extraordinary effort Disney puts into making your experience "magical", but just how far will they go to be remarkable? A recent story from the news demonstrates the level of commitment each and every Disney employee has to being extraordinary.

While on vacation at Disney's Wilderness Lodge resort, a Boston couple accidentally threw away the woman's wedding rings. They asked employees for help, but were told that finding the rings was all but impossible. The employees did however assure them that they would do what they could.

Enter "Disney Magic"! Upon investigation of the problem, the executive housekeeper realized that their trash hadn't reached the industrial-size compactor yet. He and seven other employees emptied a trash bin and sifted through bag after bag of trash until they found the rings.

Even if this story didn't have a fairy tale ending, it still would be amazing because of the remarkable effort that these employees put in to impacting the customer experience. What makes this example even more astonishing is that at Disney this is common practice. When interviewed, the executive housekeeper said "That's not the first time we've gone through trash - oh, no. We don't always find things. Many times we come up empty. But we didn't this time."

Everyday Disney employees constantly push beyond "very good" to provide extraordinary brand experiences. They don't always come out successful, but they always try. They don't say "oh what's the use." Instead, they do what needs to be done in order to make their guests' visit extraordinary.

Disney is constantly being rewarded for the efforts of its employees. Beyond this family telling this story for years to come, a secondary level of word of mouth has already begun. I saw this story on the local news this morning and at the time of writing this article, a Google search yielded over 300 pages reporting this story.

The extraordinary experience these Disney employees created further connected this family and all customers to the brand and therefore has helped to recruit more brand advocates. Would you and your employees dig through the trash for your customers? Are you willing to do to what it takes to be extraordinary? If you do, you will make an impact and your advocates will spread the word.

MYOB

Do you appreciate your elves?

My three-year-old son, Nick, was watching a children's program on PBS this morning. In the program, they told the story of the *Elves and the Shoemaker*. For those of you who don't remember the story, the shoemaker runs a small shoe business and he is very overwhelmed. He works long hours and unfortunately, no matter how hard he works, he can never earn enough money to pay the bills.

Exhausted and with nothing left in the store except a scrap of leather, he falls asleep. The next morning he wakes up early and goes downstairs to make his last pair of shoes. Much to his surprise his workbench has a pair of magnificent shoes. That day a customer enters his shop and loves the shoes so much that she gives him double the price! Now the shoemaker is able to buy leather for two pairs. The shoemaker is so happy; each morning he has enough money to buy more leather and each night the elves make more and more shoes. Before long, everyone is talking about his shop and word spreads throughout the land.

It goes on like this until the shoemaker is prosperous, however he is not satisfied. So much has been done for him yet he does not know to whom he should extend his gratitude. So one night he hides behind a curtain and as the clock strikes twelve, two naked elves hop onto the bench and begin to make the shoes. In no time, the shoes are finished and the elves, pleased with their job, dance around the shoes on the bench and leave.

The shoemaker asks himself, "How do I thank those who have made me happy and prosperous?
I know; I shall make them some clothes and shoes"
That night, the shoemaker lays out the clothes instead of leather. The elves come in, put on the clothes, dance for joy and leave, never to return. But they have given the shoemaker so much prosperity and fame that he is now able to help himself.

Like the shoemaker, you are working hard building your company. As you're looking to close the gap between your current situation and your long term vision, the important question to ask yourself is "am I creating interactions that inspire customers, employees and everyone involved with my organization to be passionately dedicated to my company and actively contribute to my success?" More importantly, you need to ask "how can I show them that I appreciate the vital role they play in my company's success?" If you do show your gratitude your passionate advocates will stick with you, unlike the elves, and continue to help you gain prosperity and fame.

Why does work have to suck?

One day, I took the commuter rail into Boston to go
to a conference. This is a trip which was very familiar
to me as I used to take this train when I worked in the
city, but this time it was different. Unlike my past trips,
I was excited and looking forward to my day. I was going to the Great Places to Work Conference which was
full of business leaders who loved where they worked
and did all they could to create organizations where
going to work is an extremely positive experience.

This was a stark contrast to what I saw around me.
Most of my fellow commuters had drained looks on
their faces and they trudged along as if they were on
a death march to an internment camp. As I walked
along with this crowd, I realized that not many of these
people had jumped out of bed and said, "Hooray, I'm
going to work today and boy will it be fun!"; at least
not without a sarcastic tone in their voice.

Why are so many work places draining the life out of
their people and what is the dysfunction of these organizations doing to the strength of these companies'
brands?

I once knew someone who was deciding between two
jobs: one that paid extremely well but would be a job
he hated, and one job that paid barely enough for him
to live on but he knew he would love. He told me of
some advice a friend gave him. "Face it, all work sucks.
I hate my job, everyone else hates their jobs, so why
do you feel you should be able to like what you do?

Therefore, you might as well take the job that pays the most because at least the money eases the pain."

With that kind of attitude do you think that person provides great customer service to his company's clients? Do you think he is constantly looking for innovative ways to improve the company's product or save the company money? Probably not. He punches his card, does what he "has to do" and gets the heck out of there as fast as he can at the end of the day. The sad thing is that a great number of workers feel the same way as him, yet most companies can't understand why their brands are losing dominance in the marketplace.

The Great Places to Work Institute develops the "100 Great Places to Work" lists and the conference I went to was full of companies that believe in creating extraordinary organizations. They all strive to develop a culture that breeds passionate advocates who share the company's vision, care about its success, strive to make the company's products truly the best and spread their passion for the brand to others both inside and outside the organization.

The results of creating extraordinary organizations were evident by all of the speakers from these Great Companies. Each one of the leaders talked about how they were the foremost brand in their particular marketplace, how their company had growth that significantly exceeded their competition as well as the stock market, but most importantly they how their people and the extraordinary culture of their organization was the cause of their brand's success.

Three days at this conference further reinforced the theory that extraordinary organizations create strong brands. So with that in mind I ask again, why are so many work places draining the life out of their people, what is the dysfunction of these organizations doing to the strength of these companies' brands, and most importantly, why does work have to suck?

Is your team ready to win?

PLAY BALL! Baseball season is about to begin. All winter, teams have been making deals to acquire the best possible talent. However, star power alone doesn't win a championship. As Babe Ruth said, "The way a team plays as a whole determines its success. You may have the greatest bunch of individual stars in the world, but if they don't play together, the club won't be worth a dime." Therefore, smart teams have spent spring training working on creating a team culture, developing team dynamics and molding their group of stars into a cohesive unit who will work together to win a championship this year.

I had the privilege to hear Red Sox skipper Terry Francona speak about the 2004 championship Red Sox. He talked about how their historic and odds defying wins were as much about team chemistry and off the field team bond as it was about on the field talent and heroics.

Companies can learn from this. When building their team, they need to examine how the talent they hire fits the culture they wish to build. It is hard to change individuals because most people don't want to critically look at themselves and they hate change. Therefore, instead of just hiring for talent, companies must examine candidates for attitude and team fit.

The entire team must be on the same page and working as a unit. An organization will fail if people are acting as individuals and in their own best interest, just like a baseball team may lose if the hitter tries to boost his batting average rather than hit a sacrifice and move the runner closer to home plate. When everyone is aligned, the organization is aligned and heading in the same direction.

Traditional business thinking aims to control situations, but companies must avoid the temptation to try to set the culture by force. Companies should stop focusing on controlling employee interactions and focus on matching up people with similar expectations who will build and deliver the desired culture. When you recruit based on shared expectations, less effort will be required to attain success. This is due to the fact that the team will shape their own culture based on these expectations and they will be inspired to advocate for the organization. Because of this, companies will find it easier to recruit and retain other loyal internal and external advocates.

If you want to win, hire for attitude and team fit, create an environment where extraordinary things can happen, give your team the power to shape the organization, the resources to get it done, and the guidance to keep it moving forward. If you follow these steps, your team will create an extraordinary culture that builds long-term advocacy, the organization will succeed, and you will have a strong and winning brand.

Do you carry out their orders?

While in high school, my first "real" job was bundling groceries for a small local grocery store chain. The job included carrying the groceries out to people's cars which at that time was becoming rare and now is almost unheard of. The job interview was one of the toughest I have ever gone through; partly because it was my first but also because of the company culture. They viewed bundling as one of the most important functions in providing the customer their brand experience.

Decades later, I still remember the expectations they laid out in the interview. Even though I was fifteen years old, I was asked how I valued customer service and how would I deliver an extraordinary experience. The lessons I learned that day set a solid foundation on which I would later develop into my current beliefs about the importance of customer service. During my training I quickly learned that everyone who touches the customer experience plays a vital role in delivering an experience which retains customers.

Then I was told the most important rules:

1. Always take care of the customer

2. Properly pack all bags so they stand up in the trunk

3. Never squish the bread

4. Under no circumstances take a tip

MYOB

After explaining the rules, they informed us that they had secret shoppers and if they caught us excepting a tip we would be fired immediately. They insisted that customers were not expected to pay more for excellent service. We were instructed to politely decline the money and inform the customers that it was our job to carry out their groceries.

They then brought me out to the exit of the store and pointed out the giant sign above the door which read, "We carry out your orders." The sign then explained the philosophy of the store and how each and every employee was expected to go above and beyond to exceed the needs of the customer. It informed customers that each employee, including bundlers, were paid to provide this level of service and customers should need not feel inclined to tip as it was part of the service the store provided to them when they chose to shop at our store.

Once I was hired, the training was more comprehensive than most of the "professional" jobs I have had. It was three days long and included classes, hands on training, and mentorship. I was instructed on proper packing technique and customer relations. By the time I flew solo I was fully aware of my role in this company, the expectations they had of me, and I had all the knowledge necessary to perform at the level their customers expected.

After I passed my probation period and proved I had what it took, I received a raise. Then I was asked if I had any friends I knew who I felt would fit in on "our team." Because I knew what they expected, I was quickly able to suggest a few good candidates as well as eliminate those who I knew would not make the cut. I appreciated the fact that management valued my judgment and took pride in helping to better "our team".

I worked for that store for eight years and I saw many changes in that time. Over the years the store merged with larger chains which were bought up by larger holding companies. The sign over the door came down, the carry-out service ended, the training was shortened to a few hours and ultimately the small-town store could no longer compete. Not because it didn't offer a selection needed to compete with the superstores, but instead because it had lost its identity, culture and ultimately its purpose. After limping along for many years, the store finally closed last year. It has been replaced in town by a large uncaring superstore and a new smaller "hometown" style market which is offering an shopping experience very similar to the one we once provided. Now they serve the shoppers we once did and people rave about shopping there.

Things have come full circle in my hometown, except for one thing: this new store doesn't carry out your orders. They did in their first few stores, but as they

have expanded the chain over the past few years they
eliminated the carry-out service in their "new" stores.
It seems the more things change the more they stay
the same and so begins the next cycle. Will they ever
learn?

Can you afford not to?

Last week, I received a disconcerting email. It was from the leader of a networking group informing us that due to the recent lack of attendance, he was moving the weekly meeting to a smaller venue. He went on to explain that most people have been citing the economy for their recent nonattendance. This got me wondering why so many businesses cut their most important brand development activities even though it is often the one thing that can help them weather a bad economic period. Despite the fact that most companies still have the resources to better their brand, they often opt to scale back their activities because they think that it will save their precious resources. By not taking advantage of prime marketing opportunities, hoarding their cash and taking a wait-and-see attitude, many companies are slowly diminishing their brand's value.

In order to grow your brand during this economic downturn, you need to strengthen your relationships, actively promote your brand, and invest in your company. Extraordinary brands are recession-proof. By following these principles, they lead the pack when the economy is good and when things go south, they survive while others die. The most important thing that top brands do best is that they don't panic. They stick to a solid strategy and keep on growing their brand no matter what state the economy is in.

During tough economic times, the first thing you need to do is stop hiding and complaining. Get out there, be visible, meet new people, and connect with new groups. When was the last time you attended an event for your Chamber of Commerce or networking group? It is always a good idea, but especially in tough economic times, to make sure you consistently strengthen your current connections, re-connect with lost connections and expand your network by leveraging the extended network of your current contacts. While you are connecting, be sure to help others make the sale. Finding opportunities for others is a top strategy for expanding your network and ultimately gaining new opportunities for yourself. When you help to connect others, they begin to value you. By helping them out, your relationship deepens and a strong relationship is the key to receiving referrals.

Next you must spread your message by advertising, sending out press releases and sponsoring events. Whatever worked in good times, do more of it in a down economy. Since times are tight, you may have limited resources and you need to get it right. So spend smart and don't spend for the sake of spending. Make sure all your promotional activity has a tangible return. A tough economic downturn is no time to simply "keep your name out there" for the sake of "building awareness." Therefore, if it is not resulting in sales activity and ultimately a sale, modify your approach but don't stop your activity. Remember there are less people buying, so now is the time where, if you can, you need to spend more, not less.

In order to grow your brand, you must invest in strengthening your company. Because most companies are cutting during tough economic times, now is the time to gain an advantage. Evaluate your entire company with an eye towards enhancement of your brand experience. If you have the resources, this is the perfect opportunity to invest in new equipment, train your people, improve your processes and procedures, re-vamp your products and services, and build your brand experience both inside and outside your organization. You may even get it all at a fraction of the cost because in a bad economy most companies are begging for your business.

This leads me to my last point; stick to your strategy. Play by your game plan, not your competition's. In any economy, but especially now, resist the temptation to deep discount in order to close the deal. Selling on price alone and discounting is a bad idea and will ultimately hurt your brand. If you keep dropping your price to undercut your competition, you may win the battle but you will lose the war. Your final rock-bottom price is probably less than you can afford to sell it for and now there is little or no profit margin left. You won the deal, but at what cost? This price may now force you to deliver a lesser product or service level. Can you even provide what the customer expects at that price? Even if you can, you have little or no resources left to deepen the relationship with that customer, let alone enough to reinvest in strengthen-

MYOB

ing your brand and attracting new customers. Don't let short-term cash undermine your long-term brand. Resist the urge to chase your competitors; set a fair price which is based on your business strategy and hold your ground. If they low ball the price, you may lose the deal but they probably won't be in business very long or will not be able properly meet the customer's expectations and in the end the integrity of your brand will win out.

If you are going to survive long-term, you need to be an extraordinary brand. During this economic downturn you may be asking yourself, "Can I afford to do all the things that are necessary to nurture my brand?" and the answer is "you can't afford not to!"

When should you spend less?

The economy is heading south, most markets are in turmoil and sales are down which means that based on conventional wisdom, now is the time for businesses to tighten their belt and spend less. When times are tough, most feel we should be spending less on marketing, putting off on buying new equipment, and postponing expanding our businesses; which is completely the wrong thing to do.

Now is the time to spend more not less. I know a business owner who is utilizing this strategy very effectively. He owns a building supply company. While the building market has dried up and his competitors are cutting back, he is spending money aggressively marketing and expanding his business. He is currently strengthening his company by adding new locations, expanding services, and buying new equipment. This is a brilliant strategy because he is able to expand his business at a bargain prices (no one else is buying from his vendors) and he can recruit top level talent from companies who are cutting back or are forced to lay people off. He also has the time to effectively train new and current employees because business is not as hectic. When his market rebounds he will be ready and he will have a competitive advantage over those who did not or could not invest in improving their businesses.

In a good economy it is fairly easy to gain and retain customers and sales often require little or no effort. Let's face it, in a booming market any monkey can make a sale because there are so many buyers. Take for example the housing boom of a few years ago: anyone with a hammer was a builder, anyone with a real estate license was selling obscene amounts of houses and anyone with a pulse was allowed to write mortgages. But now who is left? The ones who are good at what they do. Bad economies and downturn markets have a way of shaking out the bozo's. We saw it a number of years ago with the Dot-Com bust. Only the strong survived and we were left with only the extraordinary companies who had solid business plans. The fly-by-night and web developers who only got into the business because the money was great, are now extinct.

The companies who survive economic downturns are the ones who have solid business strategies and are good at what they do. However, the winners are the ones who tighten their belts during the boom and spend during the bad times. They resist the temptation to spend more than they need when the cash is pouring in. They instead put money away and invest in resources which will help them survive and possibly thrive during the rainy days. Then when things begin to slow down, they leverage their resources to improve their company and market aggressively so they are able to attract the few people who are still buying. They invest in new equipment, train their employees, and improve their processes all of which will give them a competitive edge while the market is down and when the market rebounds.

Extraordinary companies are recession-proof because they have a plan and stick to it. They tighten their belt when the economy is good and when their market dips, they grow. By following these principles, they are able to keep on thriving no matter what state the economy is in. If you are going to survive this economic downturn, you need to actively promote your business and invest in your brand. Spend as much as you can to improve your company and strengthen your place in your market. If you did not save for this rainy day hopefully you can weather the storm and learn from your mistakes. If you do survive, you now know when you should spend less and when you should invest in your brand.

MYOB

Is it better to give or receive?

"It is beginning to look a lot like Christmas every where your go," and "all the Whos in Whoville" are taking advantage of the "tremendous holiday savings throughout" the stores, buying up "the absolute best deals" on lead-painted products they can find. In companies throughout the land, the Grinch is telling his sales force to forget the holiday parties and get out there and make that final end-of-the-year sale in order to meet this quarter's quota. As the holidays approach, the Scrooges have been padding the bottom-line with massive layoffs as well as trying to squeeze the last penny of productivity and savings out of their company by shipping more and more aspects of their business overseas.

The holiday season is here yet most of us have forgotten the lesson we learned long ago that "it is better to give than receive," and because of that most of us have developed brand relationships that are very selfish. Companies think little of their customers, employees, and vendors and only focus on the bottom-line. Customers in turn have a jaded view of most brands and will switch their loyalty for a few pennies. So as the New Year approaches, what can we all do to get our brand relationships back on track?

First of all, companies need to stop focusing on just their bottom line. I am not advocating irresponsible fiscal behavior, but I am encouraging companies to build extraordinary companies that produce a healthy bottom line. Instead of sucking the life out of your organization by demanding higher profits at all costs, companies should instead focus on building an internal brand culture which creates internal advocates who believe in the organization, want to do right by the company, and help it generate a healthy bottom line.

Profit-for-profit sake only weakens the value of the brand and therefore all major financial decisions should be examined to determine how they will affect the brand long-term. What seems good for profits today may negatively affect the brand tomorrow. In contrast, a company may give up a portion of its profitability today only to receive increased brand strength in the form of customer and employee advocacy. This small act of giving will reward the company long-term and its effect is often cumulative.

As customers we must also do the right thing and support extraordinary brands. We must give up our own addiction to getting the lowest price possible. We must buy from companies who have built an organization that cares about its brand and do the right thing. As customers, we should seek out companies that are named "Great Places to Work" and care about building customer relationships. We should look for companies who are truly active in our communities and don't just give to be recognized. Lastly, we should buy our products from companies who reinvest their profits in their brands rather than line their pockets with money that should go towards building a stronger brand. By giving a few pennies extra to the good brands, we the customer will receive it back in the form of a stronger brand experience.

So as the New Year approaches we all must resolve to give a little in order to receive an extraordinary brand experience.

Do you deserve a tip?

Depending on which definition you use, the word "tips" originally stood for "to insure proper service", "to insure polite service", or "to insure prompt service". These concepts were rooted in the age old idea that individuals should be rewarded based on the level of service they provide.

Bartenders, wait staff, taxi drivers, chambermaids, and many other professions rely on tips to make a living. Many of these jobs are paid an extremely low base pay by the employer and the worker is expected to earn the remainder of their salary through tips. The idea is that the more extraordinary service they provide, the more the customer will compensate them for their effort.

One would assume that the practice of tipping would insure an extraordinary customer experience. The main problem is that these days few people provide even adequate service, yet they still expect the full tip. As customers, we are made to feel guilty leaving a low tip knowing if we don't tip well, these employees may not make a living wage.

This phenomenon of providing poor service and receiving full reward is not reserved to only tip earning professions. From the top executives down to the receptionist, the level of service all employees provide to their "customers" (both internal and external) has steadily declined over the past few decades. This decline has increased while the level of wage entitlement has risen. Workers often feel they deserve top level salaries even if they provide mediocre service.

In order to bring back extraordinary service, maybe we should revive the original tips concepts and use them to compensate all employees. From the top down to the front line employee, we should give everyone the same extremely low salary and let their "customers" both internal and external, determine the remainder of their compensation based on the level of service the worker provides. It would take the reward system away from company politics and puts it back into the hands of the people who know best, their customers. Those who are receiving service from that individual could directly compensate their service provider based on how extraordinary their experience was. This would insure "Proper, Polite and Prompt" service at all levels of an organization.

Unfortunately, having everyone work for tips is not practical but even so it does not mean we all cannot work as if we are being compensated this way. If each of us asked ourselves "Am I providing a level of service that is so extraordinary that someone would want to tip me?", maybe we would all provide our customers with a better brand experience.

What can you do to make a difference in the world?

At a business expo in Providence, RI, I had the opportunity to meet Bert Jacobs and hear him speak. Bert is the CEO (Chief Executive Optimist) of Life Is Good, a once small t-shirt company which has now become an $80 million brand with a varied product line. However, the success story of this brand is not just a financial one. Not only do they provide extraordinary products and customer experiences, but they have built a model brand with a culture that inspires a passion in both employees and customers which goes beyond their products. While employees already consider this company an extraordinary place to work, they say that their favorite part of the job is working at the many Life Is Good festivals even though they are not paid to work these events. Life Is Good holds these community-building events throughout the year to provide fun, raise money for worthwhile causes, and help to make the world a better place.

Making a difference in the world is one of Bert's corporate goals and therefore he and his brother John have built a brand with a cult-like following which inspires employees, customers and anyone who touches this company to make life good for themselves and those around them. The result is a successful company that is good for the world.

I feel more companies should be extraordinary and strive to make a difference, which is why I challenge you to make the world an extraordinary place one brand at a time. I am spreading the Life Is Good story

97

because I am passionate about creating extraordinary organizations that make a difference and this company is one model of how to do that.

I encourage you to learn more about his remarkable company by visiting *www.lifeisgood.com* or reading the many articles which have been written about them. Then use it as a catalyst to think of ways your company can be extraordinary, create passion, make a difference, and give back to the community.

Do you jump out of bed energized about your work?

Ask yourself "how passionate am I about my career."
Is it a career that energizes you each day or is it a JOB
that you drag yourself to every morning.

Do you jump out of bed full of ideas about your work?
I often do and it is not just when my alarm goes off.
I am writing this at 2:56 am because I awoke from a
dream which inspired me to write about passion.

If you are not truly energized and it is just a JOB,
then I challenge you to make a resolution to change
your organization. Everyone can become a catalyst for
building passion surrounding an organization even if
they are not the owner, CEO or even a manager.

Extraordinary things happen in organizations where
people are passionate about what they do. The sad
thing is that a great number of workers lack passion
and are full of apathy. Apathy is infectious and slowly
erodes an organization's brand, yet most companies
can't understand why their brands are losing dominance in the marketplace.

The good news is passion is contagious. Passion creates
energy surrounding a brand and that energy inspires
others including customers to be passionate advocates.
Extraordinary organizations develop a culture that
breeds passionate advocates who share the company's
vision, care about its success, and strive to make the
brand truly the best.

MYOB

Are you an advocate or a clock puncher? Clock punchers are full of apathy. They do what they "have to do" and get the heck out of there as fast as they can at the end of the day. Advocates believe in an organization. They spread their passion for the brand to others both inside and outside the organization. Overcoming apathy with passion is hard work and requires you to be an advocate.

In order to become a passionate advocate you must compare your personal mission, vision, values, objectives and goals to that of the organization.

Mission: Why we exists

Vision: Where we are going in the long-term

Values: The rules which guide us through that journey

Objectives: The milestones that need to be met to reach that vision

Goals: The specific steps that need to happen to attain these milestones

If they don't align be a catalyst for change in order to make your organization one you can be passionate about. If that is impossible get out and find an organization that fits you better. If all else fails start your own.

Let's work together to make the world an extraordinary place to work one brand at a time. I am spreading the word because it is what I am passionate about. How about you, will you jump out of bed tomorrow?

Afterword: Do you want to continue your adventure?

This collection of articles was compiled in December 2008. Since then, I have continued to write articles and each month I post them at *mindingyourownbrand.com*.

If you are interested in additional articles which encourage you think about ways to strengthen your company's brand, then I invite you to visit the site and subscribe to my monthly update.

I always enjoy discussing brand and organizational development topics with my readers. So, if you have any questions, comments, or feedback feel free to email me at dave@imageidentity.com.

* 9 7 8 1 4 4 1 4 9 4 1 7 7 *